DATE DUE

PRIMARY SOURCES OF
FAMOUS PEOPLE IN AMERICAN HISTORY™

BETSY ROSS

CREATOR OF THE AMERICAN FLAG

JENNIFER SILATE

rosen central
Primary Source™

The Rosen Publishing Group, Inc., New York

Published in 2004 by The Rosen Publishing Group, Inc.
29 East 21st Street, New York, NY 10010

Copyright © 2004 by The Rosen Publishing Group, Inc.

First Edition

Library of Congress Cataloging-in-Publication Data

Silate, Jennifer.
Betsy Ross / by Jennifer Silate. —1st ed.
    p. cm. — (Primary sources of famous people in American history)
Summary: Introduces the life of Betsy Ross, an American patriot during the Revolutionary War who enjoyed telling her family about how she sewed the first American flag.
Includes bibliographical references (p.) and index.
ISBN 0-8239-4104-3 (lib. bdg.)
ISBN 0-8239-4176-0 (pbk.)
6-pack ISBN 0-8239-4303-8
1. Ross, Betsy, 1752–1836—Juvenile literature. 2. Revolutionaries—United States—Biography—Juvenile literature. 3. United States—History—Revolution, 1775–1783—Flags—Juvenile literature. 4. Flags—United States—History—18th century—Juvenile literature. [1. Ross, Betsy, 1752–1836. 2. Revolutionaries. 3. United States—History—Revolution, 1775–1783. 4. Flags—United States. 5. Women—Biography.]
I. Title. II. Series.
E302.6.R77S57 2003
973.3'092—dc21
[B]
                                                                    2002154619
Manufactured in the United States of America

Photo credits: cover, p. 22 © Bettmann/Corbis; p. 5 courtesy of Charles H. Weisgerber II; p. 6 Rare Book Department, the Free Library of Philadelphia; pp. 7, 20 © North Wind Picture Archives; p. 8 Gloucester County Historical Society, Woodbury, NJ; pp. 9, 28 Maura B. McConnell, courtesy Betsy Ross House; p. 11 © Lee Snider/Corbis; p. 12 National Portrait Gallery, Smithsonian Institution/Art Resource, NY; p. 13 Library of Congress Rare Books and Special Collections Division; p. 14 © Hulton/Getty/Archive Photos; p. 15 Print Collection, Miriam and Ira D. Wallach Division of Art, Prints, and Photographs, The New York Public Library, Astor, Lenox, and Tilden Foundations; p. 16 Pennsylvania State Archives, Records of Pennsylvania's Revolutionary Governments (RG 27), Minutes of the Navy Board; pp. 17 (top), 23, 27 © Corbis; p. 17 (bottom) Rosen Publishing Group; p. 19 © SuperStock, Inc.; p. 21 © The Granger Collection, New York; p. 24 courtesy of Gerald Prior/Central Library, Plymouth; p. 25 courtesy of the American Philosophical Society, Records of the Society of Free Quakers; p. 29 *Harper's New Monthly Magazine*.

Designer: Thomas Forget; Editor: Jill Jarnow; Photo Researcher: Rebecca Anguin-Cohen

CONTENTS

1 YOUNG BETSY ROSS

Many people believe that Betsy Ross made the first American flag. But no one knows for sure. Whether or not she did, Betsy Ross was an unusual woman of her time.

   She was born Elizabeth Griscom on January 1, 1752. Her nickname was Betsy. She lived with her family in West Jersey, Pennsylvania. Later, she became known as Betsy Ross.

SO MANY CHILDREN!

There were seventeen children in the Griscom family. Betsy was number eight. Her family moved to Philadelphia when she was two years old.

Here is how an artist imagined Betsy Ross looked with the first American flag she sewed. This portrait is part of a larger painting.

The Griscoms were Quaker. Quakers believed in simple living. They did not believe in fighting or in war.

Quaker children did not play cards, listen to music, or dance. They played hide-and-seek and jumped rope.

Most girls in colonial times could not go to school. But Quaker girls did. At Quaker school Betsy learned to read, write, and sew.

Quaker girls were not allowed to play many kinds of games in the 1700s. But it was okay for them to jump rope like the girls in this picture.

This hand-colored engraving shows people at a Philadelphia Quaker meeting for worship. Some old Quaker meetinghouses still stand today. They are very plain and beautiful.

Betsy finished school when she was 12. She became an apprentice in an upholstery shop. Betsy lived and worked there.

John Ross was an apprentice in the same shop. Betsy and John fell in love. John and Betsy married on November 4, 1773. They opened their own upholstery shop.

Betsy Griscom married John Ross on November 4, 1773. This is their marriage license from New Jersey.

These old upholstery tools are on display in the Betsy Ross House in Philadelphia. They may not be Betsy's actual tools. But they show what her tools probably looked like.

Quakers did not allow their members to marry people from other religions. John Ross was not a Quaker. Betsy's family was very angry when she married John. Quaker law said Betsy could no longer pray in the Quaker meetinghouse. So John and Betsy Ross attended Christ Church.

DID YOU KNOW?

In church, Betsy and John sat near George Washington. They became friends. Betsy sewed shirts for him.

Betsy and John Ross attended Christ Church in Philadelphia. Built between 1722 and 1747, this church still stands in Philadelphia. It is an important landmark.

Soon after John and Betsy were married, Paul Revere came to Philadelphia. He told everyone about the Boston Tea Party. The colonists did not want to pay Britain high taxes for tea. They protested by throwing tea into Boston Harbor. Some of the colonists were dressed like Mohawk Indians.

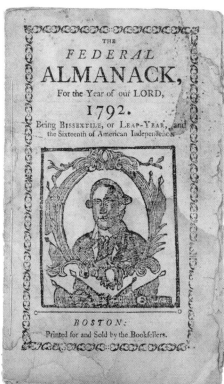

Many books called almanacs were published in the 1700s and 1800s. They included calendars, weather predictions, and other helpful information. The engraving on the cover of this almanac was drawn by Paul Revere.

Americans throwing the Cargoes of the Tea Ships into the River, at Boston

Dressed as Indians in 1773, colonists threw tea into Boston Harbor. They did not want to pay the British tax on tea. The British passed stricter laws and closed the port of Boston.

The colonists and the British began to fight the Revolutionary War. The first battles were near Boston in 1775. Betsy and John sided with the colonists. John joined the Pennsylvania militia. He guarded gunpowder. When it exploded, he was hurt badly. He died on January 21, 1776. Betsy decided to run the shop alone.

This is a picture of Colonel George Ross. Betsy Ross said that he, Robert Morris, and George Washington asked her to sew an American flag based on an idea that they had.

Amos Doolittle engraved many pictures of the Battle of Lexington and Concord. He drew his pictures based on stories told to him by people who had been there.

3 THE FIRST AMERICAN FLAG

George Washington was the leader of the colonial army. He used a red-and-white striped flag. A small British flag was in the corner. When the British saw the flag, they thought he wanted to surrender. Washington decided the colonies needed a new flag.

Shown here is a paper from the State Navy Board of Pennsylvania. It records that Betsy Ross was commissioned to make flags for navy ships. George Washington was on the flag committee.

George Washington commanded the
Continental army. This is a copy of the
flag he first used to call his troops together.
It had a British flag in the corner.

George Washington, George Ross, and Robert Morris were on the flag committee. They went to Betsy's shop with an idea for the first American flag. It had thirteen stars, one for each colony. The stars had six points. Betsy suggested using stars with five points. They agreed.

They asked her to make the flag. Betsy was very proud.

STARS AND STRIPES

Betsy's flag was adopted as the first American flag on June 14, 1777. Americans celebrate Flag Day on June 14 every year.

18

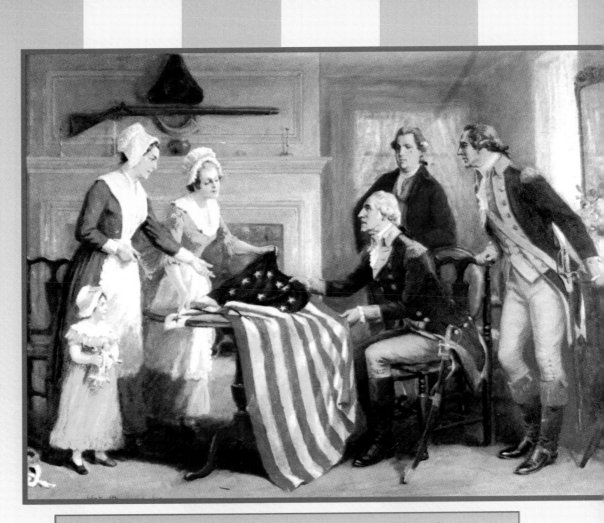

This painting shows what it might have been like when Betsy Ross presented her American flag to the flag committee.

4 SOLDIERS IN PHILADELPHIA

In 1777, Betsy married Joseph Ashburn, a sailor. He was often at sea. Betsy ran the shop.

Battles were getting close to Philadelphia. In September 1777, the British entered Philadelphia.

British soldiers took whatever they wanted from the colonists. Soldiers even moved into Betsy's house.

Colonists were forced to let British soldiers live in their homes during the Revolutionary War.

The British moved into Philadelphia and took over large homes. During the 1777 Battle of Germantown, colonists tried to force the British out. There was a bloody fight at the Benjamin Chew House. The colonists lost.

In 1778, the French entered the American war against the British. The British were afraid the French might attack New York City. They left Philadelphia to guard it.

In 1779, Betsy and Joseph's first daughter was born. Her name was Zillah. The next year, Joseph left to get war supplies. Soon after, Betsy had another daughter named Eliza.

The Marquis de Lafayette was a French nobleman. He came from France to help Americans fight against the British in the American Revolution.

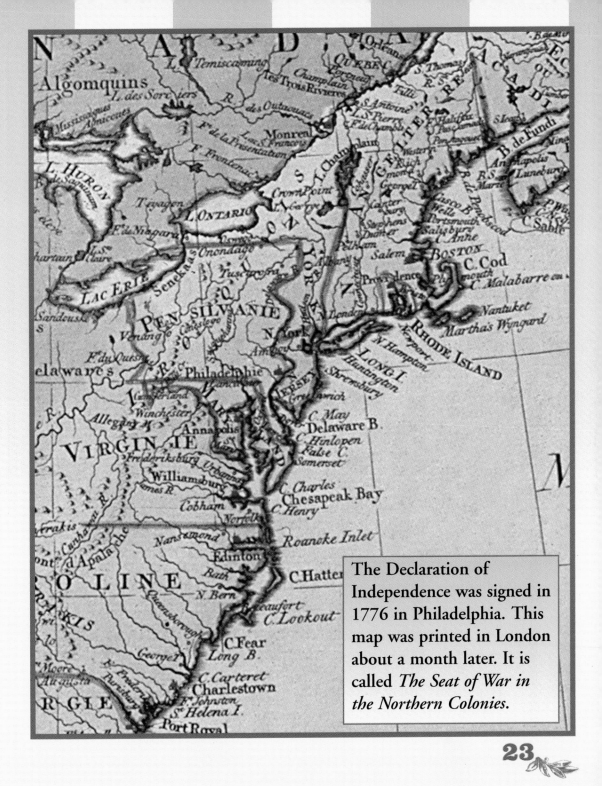

The Declaration of Independence was signed in 1776 in Philadelphia. This map was printed in London about a month later. It is called *The Seat of War in the Northern Colonies.*

5 AFTER THE WAR

The war ended in 1781. John Claypoole returned from England. He had been a war prisoner with Joseph, Betsy's husband. He told Betsy that Joseph had died.

John Claypoole and Betsy became good friends. They were married in 1783. John helped Betsy run the upholstery shop. Together they had five daughters.

Old Mill Prison, shown here, was in Plymouth, England. Living conditions there were very harsh. Betsy's second husband died in this prison. Many other American prisoners died there, too.

Betsy and John Claypoole joined the Society of Free Quakers. Also called the Fighting Quakers, they supported the American fight for independence. Betsy signed the membership book in 1785.

25

John and Betsy were married for a long time. They were always very busy.

John Claypoole died in 1817.

Betsy retired in 1827. Her daughter and a niece ran the shop. Betsy lived with another daughter.

Betsy Ross died on January 30, 1836. She was 84 years old.

RACHEL REMEMBERS MOM

"I remember having heard my mother . . . say frequently that she, with her own hands . . . made the first Star-spangled Banner."

—Betsy Ross's daughter, Rachel, in 1871

Betsy Ross rented this house from 1773 to 1786 for her upholstery shop. It still stands on Arch Street in Philadelphia. It is open for visitors.

6 BETSY'S LEGACY

Betsy Ross had often told her family how she made the first American flag. In 1870, her grandson and other relatives told Betsy's story to the Historical Society of Pennsylvania. There is no other proof.

We don't know if Betsy sewed the first American flag. One thing is certain. Betsy Ross is a true American hero.

This is the grave of Betsy Griscom Ross Ashburn Claypoole at the Betsy Ross House. It was moved here after the house became a museum.

MRS. ROSS AND THE FLAG COMMITTEE.

sary for the purpose of signals, Colonel Moultrie, who was requested by the Council of Safety to procure one, had a large blue flag made, with a crescent in one corner, to be uniform with the troops.

October 20, 1775, Colonel Reed, with the co-operation of Colonels Glover and Moylan, designed a flag or signal to be used by the American cruisers, which was adopted. It is described as a white flag with a pine-tree in the centre, and bearing the motto, "Appeal to Heaven." The London *Chronicle*, an anti-ministerial paper, contains a paragraph, January, 1776, describing a flag of this description captured with a provincial privateer at that time.

"February 9, 1776, Colonel Gadsden presented to Congress an elegant standard, such as is to be used by the commander-in-chief of the American navy, being a yellow field, with a lively representation of a rattlesnake in the middle in the attitude of going to strike, and the words underneath, 'Don't tread on me.'

"*Ordered*, That the said standard be carefully preserved and suspended in the Congress-room."

Several accounts lead to the belief that at the battle of Bunker Hill standards of various devices were used by the patriot army. From one statement we learn that "the Americans displayed a flag with the cross of St. George, the ground being blue, and in the upper corner nearest the staff a pine-tree." Another

writer says that Bunker Hill was fought under a red flag, bearing the motto, "Come, if you dare."

On the 14th of June, 1777, Congress took action, viz.: "*Resolved*, That the flag of the United States be thirteen stripes alternately red and white; that the union be thirteen stars, *white in a blue field, representing a new constellation.*" It was also proposed to insert a lyre, about which the thirteen stars were to be grouped, as embodying the "constellation Lyra," signifying harmony. But this suggestion was not carried out.

The blue field was taken from the Covenanters' banner in Scotland, likewise significant of the league and covenant of the United Colonies against oppression, and incidentally involving vigilance, perseverance, and justice. The stars were then disposed in a circle, symbolizing the perpetuity of the Union, the circle being the sign of eternity. The thirteen stripes showed with the stars the number of the United Colonies, and denoted the subordination of the States to and their dependence upon the Union, as well as equality with themselves. The whole was a blending of the various flags used previous to the war, viz., the red flags of the army and white colors of the floating batteries, the germ of our navy. The red color also, which, with the Romans, was the emblem of defiance, denoted daring, and the white purity.

The five-pointed star, from the heraldry

An 1873 article in *Harper's New Monthly Magazine* says Betsy Ross showed George Washington how to make a five-pointed star. She folded paper and made one straight cut.

29

TIMELINE

January 1, 1752—Elizabeth (Betsy) Griscom is born.

1764—Betsy becomes an apprentice in an upholstery shop.

1773—John Ross and Betsy Griscom are married.

1775—Revolutionary War begins.

1776—John Ross dies. Betsy makes the first American flag.

1777—Betsy marries Joseph Ashburn.

1779—Betsy's first child, Zillah, is born.

1782—Joseph Ashburn dies.

1783—Betsy marries John Claypoole.

1817—John Claypoole dies.

1827—Betsy stops working at her upholstery shop.

1836—Betsy Ross dies.

1870—William Canby, a grandson, makes Betsy's story known.

GLOSSARY

apprentice (uh-PREN-tis) A person who learns a trade by working for an experienced person.

colonist (KOL-uh-nist) A person who lives in a newly settled area.

Historical Society of Pennsylvania (hih-STOR-ih-kul suh-SYE-ih-tee UV pen-sul-VAYN-yuh) A group that gathers information about the history of Pennsylvania.

invade (in-VAYD) To enter a place; to attack or take over.

meetinghouse (MEET-ing-HOWS) A place where Quakers pray.

militia (muh-LISH-uh) A group of citizens who are trained to fight but who only serve in times of emergency.

prisoner (PRIZ-uhn-ur) A person who is captured or held by force.

proof (PROOF) Facts or evidence that show something is true.

Revolutionary War (re-vuh-LOO-shuh-ner-ee WOR) The war (1775–1781) in which the first thirteen American colonies won their independence from Great Britain.

surrender (suh-REN-der) To give up.

upholstery shop (uhp-HOHL-stur-ee SHOP) A store where clothes, curtains, chairs, and other things were sewn.

WEB SITES

Due to the changing nature of Internet links, the Rosen Publishing Group, Inc., has developed an online list of Web sites related to the subject of this book. This site is updated regularly. Please use this link to access the list:

http://www.rosenlinks.com/fpah/bros

PRIMARY SOURCE IMAGE LIST

Page 6: *Girls Jumping Rope*, engraving. Rare Book Department, the Free Library of Philadelphia.

Page 7: Philadelphia Quaker Meeting, hand-colored engraving, North Wind Pictures.

Page 8: Marriage license of Betsy and John Ross dated November 4, 1773. Courtesy of New Jersey, Gloucester County Historical Society, Woodbury, New Jersey.

Page 12: George Washington portrait, relief cut, from *The Federal Almanack For the Year of Our Lord, 1792*, Boston. Paul Revere, after John Norman, after Charles Willson Peale. Housed in National Portrait Gallery, Smithsonian Institution.

Page 13: *Americans Throwing the Cargoes of the Tea Ships into the River, at Boston*, engraved by W. D. Cooper in 1789. Library of Congress, Rare Books Division.

Page 14: George Ross, engraving, c. 1700, artist unknown. Courtesy of Massachusetts Historical Society.

Page 15: *Battle of Lexington and Concord*, hand-colored engraving by Amos Doolittle, created from firsthand accounts. Courtesy of Massachusetts Historical Society.

Page 16: State Navy Board of Pennsylvania minutes, May 29, 1777. Courtesy of Pennsylvania State Archives, Records of the Pennsylvania's Revolutionary Governments.

Page 17 (top): Portrait of George Washington painted by James Peale, 1760. Courtesy of Rare Books Department, the Free Library of Philadelphia.

Page 22: Portrait of the Marquis de Lafayette (1757-1834). Courtesy of Bettman/Corbis.

Page 23: *The Seat of War in the Northern Colonies*, map printed in London 1776.

Page 24: The Old Mill Prison, Plymouth, England, drawing c. 1840-1850. Courtesy Gerald Prior/Central Library, Plymouth.

Page 25: Membership book, Society of Free Quakers, 1785. Courtesy of the American Philosophical Society, Records of the Society of Free Quakers.

Page 29: An 1873 *Harper's New Monthly Magazine* article, illustrated by William Canby.

INDEX

ABOUT THE AUTHOR

Jennifer Silate lives and writes on her boat in Maryland.